THE JOURNEY TO BECOMING THE

WELL-ARMED
Woman

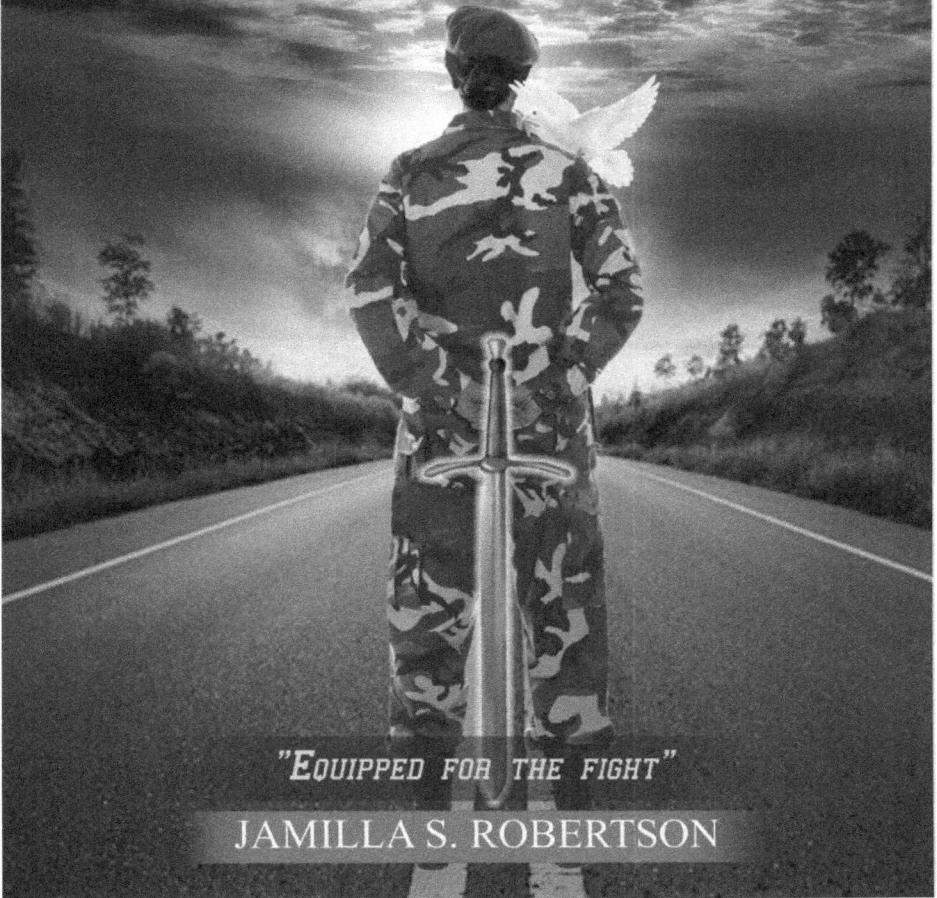

"*EQUIPPED FOR THE FIGHT*"

JAMILLA S. ROBERTSON

THE JOURNEY TO BECOMING THE

WELL-ARMED Woman

Library of Congress Cataloging-in-Publication Data

Scripture quotations are taken from the Holy Bible, New Living Translation (NIV), copyright © 1996, 2004, 2007, 2013, 2015 by Tyndale House Foundation.

Editing: SynergyEd Consulting/ synergyedconsulting.com
Graphics & Cover Design: Greenlight Creations Graphics Designs
glightcreations.com/ glightcreations@gmail.com

shero
publishing

Published by: SHERO Publishing
getpublished@sheropublishing.com
S H E R O P U B L I S H I N G . C O M

THE JOURNEY TO BECOMING THE
WELL-ARMED
Woman

JAMILLA S. ROBERTSON

THE JOURNEY TO BECOMING THE
WELL-ARMED
Woman

TABLE OF CONTENTS

BASIC TRAINING

AIT (Advanced Individual Training)

DUTY STATION

Acknowledgments

Although, you are an all-wise, all-powerful, make no mistake Heavenly Father, I couldn't help but wonder if You had the right person when this assignment came down the pipe for me to write this book. I can't praise You enough for this journey. Thank you, Jesus! I can now see Your hand of mercy is ALWAYS on my life. I submit every fiber of my being back to you.

To my dearest Darrell, you've opened my eyes and heart to real love. Love that has no boundaries and no conditions. I'm thankful that your shoulders are made of massive buckets to hold all the tears that I've cried on them. Your encouraging words always make me feel like I can truly conquer the world. I love you with all of my heart.

To my two hearts outside of my chest, Jamya and Marti, you make me so proud to be your mommy. You two have hung in here with me through one of the toughest parts of my journey. I know you have prayed many silent prayers for me, and I am forever grateful for such amazing kids.

To my bonus babies, Dynasty and Nisir, you've received me and respected me from the beginning of our blended family journey. I appreciate every laugh, every encouraging word, and every heartfelt hug I continuously receive from you two.

To my Aunt Maria and my cousins/brothers, Quenton and Nishaun, "We all we got!" Our family may be small in number, but our love for one another is huge. Thank you for always having my back and believing in me.

To my bestie, Stacey, you are the epitome of what a real sister is supposed to look like. You can attest to well over twenty years of my journey, and you never turned your back on me. I appreciate and love you more than you will ever know!

To my dearest friend/sister Lashaunda, you have always "made my baby leap." I praise God for such a genuine soul entering my life when I most needed a spiritual sister to lean on. You have seen me weary many times and continue to hold my arms up like Aaron did Moses. I know victory belongs to us because we have found our **REAL** Daddy.

To all of the sisters of my *Sisters, Let's Giv'em Something to Talk About* women's group, past, present, and future to come, your continuous showing up has helped and pushed me much more than how often you all say that I've helped and pushed you. Thank you for believing in me and taking a lap of my journey with me. The best is yet to come!

Thank you to my SHERO Publishing family/coaches, Erica, Kim, Sharonette, and Chemeka. We've finally come to the end of this segment of my journey. You all have made "birthing this baby" extremely painless. I couldn't have gotten this completed without your constant push and encouragement.

Lastly, to all of my mentors, spiritual leaders, and pastors, thank you for your Godly wisdom and constant prayers anytime I've ever come and sought advice. You've always told me the truth, whether I wanted to hear it or not.

Foreword

It is an honor and a privilege to introduce you to the amazing Jamilla Robertson and *The Journey to Becoming a Well-Armed Woman*. My journey with Jamilla dates back many years to us playing in our cousin's backyard as children and walking into our teen years, struggling to find our identity. We were distant cousins with remarkably close secrets. The source of the secret may have been different, but the similarity of feeling the need to prove something was always lurking in our midst.

The book you are holding in your hands is not a "how-to guide" for learning how to dress in armor; it is a very transparent and personal peek into how Jamilla has become armed and dangerous! She shares her inner secrets, she pulls back the veil on her pain, and she allows you to visit the most vulnerable pieces of her heart. What you are reading is a compilation of her pain being squeezed into purpose and her prayers propelling her toward destiny.

The Journey to Becoming A Well-Armed Woman will give you permission to evaluate your present life based on the path that led you to your current position in life while granting you consent to ask God the really hard questions. Jamilla's experiences teach us that God is not intimidated by our questions, in fact, He yearns for us to ask them so that He can continue to direct us according to the plan He has for us, even when we venture off track.

I have had an up-close and personal view into many of the seasons that Jamilla shares in this book, and I can honestly say she is well armed and committed to arming you. If you apply the life lessons in this book, you will experience an inner transformation that makes your heart smile and brings God glory. You will be dressed and ready to do battle as you fight to experience God's best for your life. Be warned, this book will challenge you to confront and arm the person who has the most impact in your life – you.

Keisha B. Spivey
Executive Director
Community Pastor

Introduction

Have you ever said yes to a particular situation or circumstance and not fully understood all that the "Yes" entailed? Of course! That is exactly how this project came about. I accepted Christ as the Lord and Savior of my Life in my early 20s. Saying yes to Him completely changed my life forever in ways I couldn't even fathom were possible.

I can remember having a one-on-one session with my mentor, Keisha, in 2013, when she had me do a "Do-Be-Have" list. This list consisted of things I wanted to do, things I wanted to be, and things I wanted to have. Much thought, prayer, and consideration went into this list. Nothing too small or too big was exempt from making the list.

While many things, over time, have been crossed off the list, many things have yet to be completed on the list. After praying one day, the Lord had me add *Author* to the list of things I wanted to be. I hesitated, thinking, *surely, Lord, you're not telling me to write a book.* I dismissed this assignment many times as He reminded me to complete this. Of course, He always has a way of making things louder to me until I give in to obedience, so here we are.

I invite you to take a glimpse of my journey to becoming a *Well-Armed Woman*. Every journey has a destination. We may not always understand the destination initially, but somewhere along the journey, it will become clear where our final destination will be.

As I share bits and pieces of my journey with you, my prayer is that you will take inventory of your personal journey to see how it parallels or even brings things to your remembrance about your journey.

While my journey to becoming a well-armed woman is an evolving process, it is just that, a process. I'm here to tell you, don't fight your process, don't despise your process, and don't forfeit your process. Accept it. Embrace it. And most definitely flow with it because this part of your journey will lead you to become the *Well-Armed Woman* YOU were predestined to be. Now, turn the page and take this journey with me. YOU ARE EQUIPPED FOR THIS FIGHT WHETHER YOU REALIZE IT OR NOT!

THE JOURNEY TO BECOMING THE

WELL-ARMED
Woman

THE JOURNEY TO BECOMING THE

WELL-ARMED
Woman

BASIC
TRAINING

It Was a Fight from the Beginning

The fight started the day I entered the earth. You see, I was an only child born to a thirty-year-old woman who had her own list of struggles before me. My mother was diagnosed as bipolar, and as far back as I can remember, she was on medication to assist in controlling it.

Growing up in the house with my mommy, I never understood the disorder she was suffering from. All of a sudden, she would have an episode where her mood would shift. She'd go from being happy to deep sadness without any warning. When these moments occurred, she would sometimes have fits of rage, uncontrollable crying, sink into a deep depression, or respond like a little infant child. There were sporadic occasions where she would have to visit the hospital to get back on track. I now know the hospitals she visited were occasionally mental institutions. These episodes didn't occur very often, but when they did, they were most memorable. Due to my age, my family never really explained mommy's illness to me. I recall hearing words like *nervous breakdown, bipolar, anxiety,* and even the word *crazy*. I never identified with what triggered her. I knew if she took her medications regularly, she was fine.

I can remember periods where she would get frustrated with taking the medication and would stop altogether in hopes of getting better on her own. A sure indication that she had stopped taking her medicine was when an episode would rear its ugly head.

Occasionally, my family could convince her to start the medicine back. Other times, she would have to go to the hospital or mental institution to have the medications forced back into her system. Even though she suffered from this illness, she made sure I had everything I needed and much of what I wanted, regardless.

I will forever remember my mommy as a beautiful, hard-working, classy, and elegant woman. She appeared as a giant to me when I was a little girl, but in reality, she was about 5'11" tall, a very statuesque woman. She graduated high school in NC and soon left for New York City to pursue a modeling career. She remained in NY for many years, modeling, working, and chasing her dreams. We talked and laughed together often. Let me tell you, her laugh was horrible, by the way. It was a very high screeching pitch, but I couldn't help to want to hear it over and over again.

She taught me many principles of conducting myself as a lady. She would say to me often, "Jamilla, you have on a dress. How are you supposed to sit?" I knew how to set the table long before I had the home economics class in grade school. Our favorite pastime was shopping. I was exposed to high-end fashion at an early age. We went to Broadway plays, took family vacations, and visited plenty of parks and playgrounds.

Birthdays were huge to us because she instilled in me that it was a blessing to see another year. We even often dressed alike. Because she was a model, always ready for photo opportunities, there were plenty of pictures to capture our happy moments.

I was constantly transitioned from Brooklyn, New York (which is where I was born), to North Carolina, to my maternal grandparents, who lived in a small town called Nashville; much of my life was spent there. Normally, I went to school in North Carolina, and I spent my summer vacations in New York.

Though my family did their best to provide me with everything, I had my share of hurt and pain that no one in this world could have ever prepared me for. The Grim Reaper started visiting my family, and the deaths started coming back-to-back.

I never really had a relationship with my biological father or his side of the family. Growing up, my mother and her side of the family was the only family I knew. I was about eight years old when my grandmother received a phone call that shook us to the core. My grandfather had gone fishing earlier that morning and was found slumped over his steering wheel. He had passed away of an apparent heart attack. That was my first-time experiencing death, but it definitely would not be my last. Two years later, on the anniversary of my grandfather's death, my grandmother took her last breath. On the exact same day! I can remember feeling so empty. Other than my mother, the two most important people in my life were now gone.

Mama Prepared Me for This

My mother decided to relocate back to Nashville, NC. I was in the seventh grade at that time. She and I lived in my grandparent's home and were happy as we could be from what I could tell. In NY, my mother worked for American Express for well over twenty years. She did very well for herself. When we transitioned to North Carolina permanently, she liquidated her savings account and her retirement fund. I didn't understand the sacrifice she made for us, namely me.

I noticed that we started to struggle financially. Apparently, the funds were depleted. We were getting government assistance, including food stamps. My mother worked as a substitute teacher to help make ends meet. By now, I was reaching my teenage years when I was hit with yet another blow. My mother was diagnosed with breast cancer.

I could not fully understand the impact this was getting ready to have on us, but we were soon in the clutches of an unforgiving reality. She ended up having a double mastectomy, and we thought she was on the road to recovery. As we began to get back to our normal lives, my mother was informed that the cancer that was once in her breast had now spread to other organs in her body. She was given about six months to live.

My mother was a woman of faith and appeared to have accepted what was about to take place. She always had my best interest in mind despite all of her aches and pains she was experiencing. On top of all that, she was still dealing with bipolar disorder, type II diabetes, asthma, and congestive heart failure. Nevertheless, she was adamant about me going to college after graduating high school.

I'll never forget the events leading up to her transition from earth to glory. My mother and I were home alone as usual. She was having a bad day and had to have a lot of help at home. She laid down to retire for the night but later had to get up to use the bathroom. Not wanting to bother me, she got up alone and fell and bumped her head on the tub. She had been there for a while before she mustered up the strength to yell out for me. I jumped out of bed and ran to her aid. She was mumbling and unable to speak clearly. The doctors believed that she might have had a stroke. I helped her back to bed and called my aunt. My aunt dialed 911, and the emergency responders were on the way. That was her last trip to the hospital. During this stay, she was still not speaking clearly. Her words were just mumbles that no one could understand.

On the day of her transition, she began to talk again. She requested the nurses to contact me. The nurses called my two aunts to make them aware of my mother's request. When we reached the hospital, she requested to see me alone. As a fifteen-year-old without much understanding of what was going on, I took her talking again as a miracle, and my mother was on her way back home. That was not the case, though.

During our private conversation, she informed me of all the whereabouts of her important papers, such as life insurance policies, written obituary, and final requests. She told me that she had to move them to a different location because a few people were trying to get her to sign everything over to them and vowed that they would take care of me after she was gone. We also talked about my living arrangements with my aunt, uncle, and cousin after she transitioned. She emphasized that she really wanted me to go to college after high school, and she wanted me to do good with the rest of my life. She explained that I had plenty of time for boys and babies.

As she laid there giving me her rundown of my life, she looked so peaceful. I couldn't grasp why she was making all these declarations. In my mind, God had answered my prayers, and she was healed. We were going home to live happily ever after. We exchanged many more words, and the last thing we declared to each other was our love for one another as I kissed her on the forehead.

Afterwards, I rejoined my family downstairs in the main lobby. My aunts then went upstairs to visit her, and guess what? She was not speaking clearly again. Her words were back to mumbles. My aunts were in disbelief as I was telling them what she and I talked about. I was confused as to what just happened. No explanation was given to me either. By the time we reached home, the phone was ringing. My sweet forty-five-year-old mother had gone on to be with the Lord.

This happened the summer before I entered the eleventh grade. *How in the world am I going to live without my mother for the rest of my life? You mean to tell me she isn't going to see me walk across the stage at my high school or even college graduation? You mean she will never see her grandchildren whenever they would be born into this world?* I had an extremely difficult time digesting this.

I became angry that I was experiencing this so early in my life. I looked at many of my friends and classmates, and everyone else had their mother. Having to grow up without my mother really took a toll on my life. There was so much I missed out on, so much she never got to share with me. No one sat me down and told me about the life lessons I should have known about, like money matters, relationship matters, matters of the heart. The absence of my father left me searching for more than just a father's presence. I was looking for love in all the wrong places. I became very promiscuous, trying to compensate for the lack of validation, affirmation, and value that the impartation of a father has in the life of his daughter.

Looking back, some thirty-plus years later, I can see God's hand of mercy was **always** on my life. At fifteen years old, I did not know or have a relationship with Christ. I had not asked Him to be my personal Savior, but His grace was covering me when I didn't even realize it. I'm a firm believer that I had a praying mother whose prayers God remembered, even when I didn't remember Him.

I share my beginning journey with you because we don't always have control of the various situations or circumstances that occur in our lives, but we don't always have to end up on the bad end of the deal. In the end, there was her plan for my life, and then there is His plan for my life. If we allow, His plan will always supersede any other plans. I am forever grateful for my family that was in place during all of this, but as I grew older and started to mature more, I had to figure out for myself what the rest of my life was going to look like without her.

As I approached my high school graduation, I knew this was my time to begin again with a clean slate. What was next for my life was going to shape and change the rest of my life. The journey continues.

Daddy, Where are You?

I have heard many say, "I grew up without a father and turned out fine." Well, that may be the case for me now, but it was certainly a difficult process to get to this place. The times where I was living in Brooklyn with my mother didn't make me miss my absent biological father much at first. As I was flipped flopped from New York to North Carolina, my granddaddy was present in my life in Nashville, NC, but there was no father figure present in Brooklyn. My mother was single. She dated men from time to time but never remarried. "Where is my daddy?" I began asking my mom as his absence became more and more apparent to me. I remember seeing pictures of him. I was a very small child, about one or two years old, sitting in his lap along with my mommy. I wasn't old enough to have any memorable times with him. I was told that he and my mother were married at one time. By the time I knew of him, he was long gone.

In Nashville, we lived on a noticeably short street, Ward Street, about a half-mile long. This small community was full of little girls, like me, with their families. We were all about the same age. I was in elementary school, about the third grade, when I began to observe that all my friends that lived on my street had parents -- a mom and a dad. I guess I was okay with all of this until my grandfather passed away. I was still doing my rotation between NY and NC. Now, there was no father in my life at all. My two aunts were married at the time. One of my uncles was in the Marines and stationed in California. My Uncle Adolph, the one I lived with after my mother passed away, worked six days a week, so I rarely saw him until I started living with my aunt, cousin, and him.

One summer in Brooklyn, I must have gotten on my mother's nerves with all the questions about my father. His name was Joseph Robertson, also known as Joe.

"Where is my daddy? Where is my daddy, mommy?" This question went on periodically for some time without an answer.

Finally, a response, "Do you want to meet your father?"

"YES!" I screamed.

We got dressed, she made a phone call, and we were on our way. We took off walking.

I started to get confused because if we were going a long distance, we would normally take a cab, a bus, or the subway, sometimes all three depending on the distance. Nope, not this time. We just kept walking. It was a lengthy walk, but that was not very uncommon in the city. We made one more turn, crossed a street, and entered into a small corner store.

"Your daughter has been asking about you," my mommy said to this tall, slim man that I noticed I resembled.

"Hey, baby! Come here and give me a hug," the man stated.

Well, come to find out, the man was Joe, my father. He was an older gentleman. My birth certificate states that he was forty-five years old when I was born, but my Aunt Maria swears he was much older than that. He was about 6'5 or 6'6 tall, slim build with a small salt and pepper afro.

You must remember, this was the mid-1980's, so afros were in style then. I now saw where I got my height from, although my mom was taller than most women too. He was working in this small store that my mom and I conveniently walked to. He worked there for many years and even lived above the store in a small apartment.

The corner store sold your everyday whatnots like sodas, juice, chips, candy bars, newspapers, magazines, ice cream, etc. I later found out that this store was just a front (cover-up) for what was really going on. They ran numbers (illegal lottery) out of the back of the store. There was always a steady stream of customers flowing through there on a daily basis, but everybody wasn't buying candy bars and soft drinks, if you know what I mean.

Now the people in the store knew him personally and began to compliment him on his beautiful little girl. "Oh Joe, she's so pretty! She looks just like you!"

He just stood there soaking it all in like he was the man of the hour. I distinctly remember during this whole ordeal as I was thinking to myself, "WE WALKED HERE! WE...WALKED...HERE! We didn't take a bus, a cab, the subway. We walked here!" My mommy and I walked to this man that I never remembered seeing nor had a conversation with over the telephone. I never received any gifts from him for birthdays, holidays, back to school, nothing. That, to me, was a clear indication that I wasn't important to him. I mean, we've been that close to him my entire life, and he didn't even bother to reach out to me, not that I knew of.

My next thought was, why? *Why don't we have the father-daughter relationship that I had yearned for? Why has he not reached out to me all this time? JUST WHY?* All of this was running through my mind as he was standing there pleading for this hug. I finally got close to him and leaned in, and gave him a real fake hug. You know, the one-arm hug you give to a person when you really don't want to. I don't recall much that happened that day after my initial meeting with him.

From then on, he was Joe. I never called him father or daddy. His name was Joe until the day he took his last breath on this earth. I felt like that was a title that had to be earned, and he never earned either of those titles from me. My granddaddy was my daddy, and he was no longer with me. Joe never minded me calling him by his first name either. I guess he knew he hadn't been much of a father to me.

After my mommy and I moved to North Carolina permanently, Joe attempted to have somewhat of a relationship with me. I was no longer visiting Brooklyn for the summers. He was a huge liar, though. I would contact him like any other little girl would do to ask for help with something, and he would always tell me some story as to why he couldn't, or he sent it, but it must've gotten lost in the mail.

One time, he told me he forgot to put a stamp on it, and it came back to him. Even after he received it back, I never received whatever he said he sent to me. Rarely, I mean, every blue moon, my mommy would get some money from him through the mail. He did make a guest appearance when my mother passed away. He attended her funeral, handed me $200, and was on the next thing smoking back to New York.

My mother was gone. My father was not there for me. Regardless, from this point on, I knew that I had a promise to keep. My mother wanted the best for me. She did her best for me. Now I had to take everything that she imparted in me and find my way. However, it would've been nice if Joe had stepped up to the plate and been more active in my life.

I must admit, there were more conversations over the phone. I even visited him a couple of times and worked in his store to earn some extra money to go clothes shopping as I prepared for my senior year of high school. From the ages of 15 to 18, we made several attempts to communicate better, but that never quite filled the void I longed for.

I was always puzzled because Joe had a son, my half-brother, Sidney. I never knew him personally, but we did get to meet him two times. I was in the military by the time we met. What I found out later that Sidney was sick with cancer. Sure enough, not much longer after we met the second time, I got a phone call from Joe stating that Sidney had passed away. I think meeting me was something he wanted to do before he died.

I could tell that this was a devastating blow to Joe. It was apparent that he had a better relationship with Sidney than he had with me. I did the right thing and attended the funeral with Joe. His heart was broken, and he kept stating to me that burying a child was the hardest thing he ever had to do. It seemed to have worried him so much that about two months after Sidney's death, Joe fainted in his store. He had suffered a brain aneurysm. I made one last visit to NY to see him in the hospital.

As he laid there with all types of tubes attached to him, we shared what I believed was the realest moment of my 18 years. I declared to him that I forgave him. I forgave him for not being present in my life when I needed and wanted him to; for the lies he always told me; for pretty much abandoning me; and for not stepping up when my mother passed away.

I also asked him for his forgiveness. I didn't always have nice words to say to him when I was in my feelings about our relationship. I ended the conversation with an I love you and a kiss on his forehead. He was unable to speak because of the tubes, but I could tell my words were received by the tears coming out of his eyes. About two weeks later, yep, you guessed it. Joe was gone.

There are many things that life just doesn't prepare you for. Losing my grandparents, my mother, a half-brother, and my father didn't prepare me for the journey I was enduring. Not to mention, I was starving for the love of a father that I never received until I accepted Jesus Christ into my life. YET, I will survive. The journey continues.

The Choice

The loss of my mother is something I know I will never get used to. I'll never really get over it. Oh, how I love and miss my mother. The time had come. I was a senior in high school, and decisions had to be made. Would it be college? I know this is what my mother always wanted for me. Now was faced with even more questions. Is this what I want for myself? How can I afford it? Who's going to pay these fees, my tuition? The responsibility of making these decisions and trying to figure out how it was going to get done became very overwhelming to me. Although I had the support of my aunt and uncle, the burden of my future was not something I wanted to place on anyone.

I went walking through the neighborhood as I would on any given day, and I ended up at my girlfriend's house. To my surprise, there was a recruiter from the United States Army there talking with her about joining. He shared with us about the many benefits and opportunities joining the Army would bring to one's life. So, not only would I have the opportunity to serve my country, but I would also be able to make my own money to support myself, have medical benefits, travel the world, and they were even going to pay for me to go to college too!

BLING! The light bulb came on. I could keep my promise to my mom. This recruiter was laying it on thick. Everything he said sounded like the answers to my unspoken prayers. So, I was all in. I said, "Yes" to Uncle Sam! A senior getting ready to graduate from high school, I was only seventeen. So, even though I said yes to going into the military, I wasn't old enough to make that decision on my own, so I had to get a parent's signature to enlist.

The only parent I had was my sometime present father. You mean to tell me that I have to get permission for my future from a man who really played no role in my life? So, I reached out to Joe to share with him the choice I had made for my life. He was not really in agreement, having served himself. He tried to talk me out of it, sharing his thoughts, insight, and opinion. At the end of the day, it was my life, my decision, and all I needed was his signature. Against his better judgment, he signed it. *I'm going to the military!*

I'm not at all sure what I've signed up for. All I know is I will be positioned to financially take care of myself, travel the world, and fulfill my promise to my mother and go to college. Graduation can't come fast enough. I'm ready for my new journey to begin. After graduation, it was time to report to basic training. Fort Jackson, South Carolina, here I come. The journey continues.

The Harsh Reality of My Choice

I graduated from high school, my dad signed the papers for me to enlist in the military, and it was now time to leave for basic training., I remember getting on the bus bound for Fort Jackson, SC. Here is where I would report for basic training. The ride was dark and intense. We rode the bus into the wee hours of the morning. I didn't know what to expect.

When we arrived, the driver opened the door, "Fort Jackson, South Carolina!" he yelled with a bit of I feel sorry for you all in his voice. *We're here! Let the journey begin*, I thought to myself with excitement. What came next quickly let the air out of my balloon. All I heard was loud voices of the drill sergeants yelling and screaming for us to fall in line. *What is this? What the heck have I gotten myself into?*

At that moment, all I could think about is I wish my mama were here. Well, she was not, I was there, and this was my choice. Good or bad. Like it or not. This was now my reality, and I had to figure it out, like everything else in my life.

One thing that became very clear, very quickly, is that the recruiter had deceived me. The harsh reality is that there was nothing basic about my basic training—eight grueling weeks of non-stop training on becoming a soldier and preparing for combat. There were times I wanted to quit. I wanted to give up. Yet, I kept remembering my mother. I couldn't let my mother down. Quitting was no longer an option. Besides, I had one of the greatest examples of a fighter I can remember, and that was my mother.

Although life ended way too soon for her, I watched my mother fight in my 15 years of life. She fought to provide and to take care of me as best she could. Even on her death bed, when at one point she couldn't even talk, she fought to tell me all she wanted me to know—always thinking about me. Fighting for me. Rest on, Mom. You fought well. Now, it's my turn to fight. Fight for the future. I know you so wanted for me. Basic training was designed to create the fabric that will shape and mold my future as a member of the United States Army. Bring it on, basic training. I'm from Brooklyn, New York, by way of Nashville, NC, and there is nothing basic about me.

Take the Journey...

My life was purposed, so was my journey:

Jeremiah 29:11 "For I know the thoughts I think towards you, thoughts of peace and not of evil. To give you a hope, a future, and an expectant end."

Every journey has a place from which it starts. While our journeys and process may differ, our desires are the same, to be whole and complete, nothing broken, nothing missing. Let's explore some events along your journey that may have played a role in building the foundation from which you started.

1)What are some of the life experiences that have navigated your journey or charted your basic training?

_____

_____

_____

_____

_____

2) As you reflect on your life, what are some life-molding memories or nuggets you and your mom have shared?

_____

_____

_____

_____

_____

3) There's a saying that says, "You can't miss what you never had." But that saying isn't true when what you've missed is having your dad. What impact has having, or not having, your dad in your life had on your life?

_____

_____

_____

_____

_____

THE JOURNEY TO BECOMING THE

WELL-ARMED
Woman

A.I.T.
Advanced Individual Training

Orders Received

Basic training was eight of the longest weeks of life. I was in unfamiliar territory, with people I didn't know, embracing a journey no one prepared me for. At this point, I couldn't tell if I had made the best decision or worst mistake of my life. When the Army slogan says, "We do more before 9:00 AM than most people do all day!" That's the absolute truth!

South Carolina's heat in July was not kind. We were up before the sun even thought about peeking through the sky. There was constant physical training that consisted of pushups, sit-ups, and daily running that had me in the best shape of my life. We also received constant training of "just in case we are attacked" scenarios. Remember, I was only 17 years old. Handling grenades and firing an M16 rifle was becoming my new norm. Falling asleep in class only resulted in more extensive PT (physical training) as punishment. Let's just say, I was in amazing shape when it was all said and done.

I made it! It's graduation day, basic training is over, and I am looking forward to seeing my family members, like my aunt, uncle, and several of their friends who traveled to support me. They were proud of me, and I was proud of myself too. I am sure there were many that thought I wouldn't make it. If I can be honest, there were times I didn't think I would either. All I had to hold on to was my determination to keep my promise to my mother.

Well, the "Big Day" has come, and I've received my orders. The envelope, please! Where oh where will I go from here? I went straight from Basic Training to AIT in Fort Leonard Wood, Missouri. That's right, Missouri! I had to look up Missouri on the map to see where it was located. By the time I arrived, the weather was changing to a much cooler climate, yet, the physical training of this journey continued more pushups, sit-ups, and running.

My basic training was with all girls, except for my drill sergeants. I immediately notice that my AIT was going to be a Coed venture. Here I am, this seventeen-year-old black girl from New York, City by way of Nashville, NC, not even old enough to vote, but yet being prepared for war.

I am sure you may be wondering, what is AIT? It stands for Advance Individual Training. If Basic Training was where the foundation I received was laid, then AIT is where the building would be erected, and the US Military Solider I had become would be skillfully trained as a 88M (Mike), Motor Transport Operator, or more commonly known as a truck driver. I learned much of what there was to know about trucks: how to drive one, how to identify the different ones I would operate, the basic mechanics of them, and how to identify issues in the event one should occur. I was being trained specifically for my next assignment, my permanent duty station.

Unlike basic training where everyone was trained together from all departments and divisions of the US Army, AIT was more assignment-focused, including the "what to do in case we're attacked" scenarios and the physical training. These drill sergeants were strict, but they didn't do as much yelling as they did in basic training. As the five weeks quickly passed, I grew in knowledge and skills. I was equipped and ready for service.

It was so rewarding for me to have successfully completed Basic Training and AIT. Now here I am, a US Army soldier, Motor Transport Operator, ready, trained, and equipped for the next phase of my journey.

After successfully completing basic training and AIT, many go on to their permanent duty stations if they enlisted full-time or returned home if they were only part-time (Reserves). Me, I was all in. Full-time soldier me, please.

"Private Jamilla Robertson, Fort Eustis!"

For a moment, I thought I was off to Texas. "Ummmmm, drill sergeant, where is that located?" I softly asked.

"Virginia, soldier!" he declared.

My permanent duty station was only going to be 2 hours away from home. God had truly favored me.

I was getting settled in my new home, the barracks of my new company at Fort Eustis, Virginia. Guess what? I was still only a 17-year-old private. I had been in the Army a whole six months before my 18th birthday. My permanent duty station is where I would complete my military time of three years I had enlisted for.

I turned 18 years old in November 1992, and in January 1993, we were deployed to Africa, Operation Restore Hope. *Surely, I'm too young to go to a real war!* Nope, Uncle Sam didn't think so. It was time to put all of those "just in case" scenarios into full effect. This was real-life gunfire and real-life attacks on our lives.

You would think because my training was so fresh, I would remember what to do. It was a completely different ball game when I was engulfed in these situations in real-life. It was the most memorable, scary, and life-changing moment of life. I was determined to make it home and not in one of those black body bags.

Our deployment lasted about six months. As a transportation specialist, we were constantly in danger as we did various driving assignments throughout Somalia, Africa. Each time seemed more dangerous than the last assignment. Returning home completely changed my outlook on life. I immediately concluded that this soldiering thing was not for me. I anxiously completed my military time in July 1995, and I gave Fort Eustis, Virginia, and the US Army the peace sign.

Reflecting on my military tenure made me realize that each phase of my journey prepared me for the next phase. There was no way I could enter a real war without going through the proper training/preparation. As we journey through life, we can see how each piece of our lives, both the good and the bad, fits nicely together into the large puzzle. This puzzle will not be completed until we take our last breath. The journey continues.

I Do! (The Marriage)

Returning home to North Carolina was no walk in the park. I was clueless as to what a soldier like me would do now, that I was back in civilization. Face it, I went straight into the military after high school; it was all I knew. The military was my first job ever. I never worked as a teenager, like so many of my other friends in high school. Yet, I knew I had to do something.

I had a few jobs, here and there, but nothing really held my attention. I was anxious to see if all of this given of myself to the Army for all those years actually paid off. Remember, my number one reason for enlisting was to get financial assistance for college. Sure enough, the Army assisted me financially with college. I also ended up joining the National Guard. I did that for three years, this time only part-time, one weekend a month.

During my last year in the National Guard in 1999, I met my then-husband. We enjoyed each other's company. We laughed, loved, and dreamed out loud, sharing our goals, dreams, and aspirations. He was the one, so I thought.

After dating for about a year, we got married in 2001. Although my family was not in agreement with my choice, they supported my decision. Well, "I's Married Now!" and I so looked forward to all of our goals and dreams manifesting. Life was good, at least from the exterior of it.

On April 23, 2003, I gave birth to our daughter, our firstborn. Wow! Me, a wife, a mom. It was so overwhelming, as this was never the fairytale ending I experienced growing up as a child, but it is one I always wanted. Our daughter was the love of our lives, and I knew now that nothing would keep us from reaching our goals and bringing our dreams to life. We had someone else motivating us.

As I look back over that time in our lives, my life, I remember reflecting a lot about the times my mother and I shared. I couldn't wait to share some of those precious moments with my daughter like my mother had shared with me and at the same time vowing to protect her at all cost from some of the things my mother couldn't protect me from because of the struggles she had. I would be strong for my daughter, just like my mother was for me, even down to her taking her very last breath.

By January of the following year, I was pregnant again. While my aunt and uncle, who took me in after my mother died, was excited about me giving them grandchildren, they weren't so supportive of the choice I made in a husband who would go on to father our children.

Little did I know, while I was busy trying to cover up and compensate for my husband's shortcomings, my family saw straight through it.

On October 1, 2004, our son was born. I was given a man child from the Lord! Our family had expanded yet again, and I just knew things would get better. They had to! We now had two children we were responsible for. Surely, our goals and dreams would come to pass now. He would have to step up to the plate, rise to the occasion, and be the man he perpetrates being.

I had been very supportive. We were very active in our church. He was called to preach but had not yet yielded to his Call. Until he did, the way he sang would grab the attention of the angels, and I was right there standing by his side, supporting him. During this time, I accepted my call to preach even though he had not yet accepted his. God was using me mightily. This would become a problem for us. I believe, because of this, he allowed the spirit of jealousy to come between us. We were professionals at maintaining our public look of success, even though I knew we were privately failing.

Who am I kidding? Our marriage became toxic, unhealthy and infidelity had crept right on in. I was married to a master manipulator who had to be seen as in control, but our lives and finances were out of control. We were not responsible stewards over what God entrusted to us. We lost homes, cars, and so much more. I lost sight of my own identity.

Our lives were spiraling out downward. We had lost everything. Me, my husband, and our children were now calling the local Motel Six our new home. Very few knew it. I was running a business from it and everything. I remember putting together an event while living in the motel. What should have been a success turned out failing because while the resources had come in for the event, I was using portions of the money to keep us in the motel, which played a major part in the event falling apart.

I'll never forget when Christmas came around. We stayed with one of my girlfriends because we didn't have a home to celebrate in, and I didn't want our children to celebrate in the motel. Yes, it was official we were the public success and private failure the world and my family would come to know about.

When I said I do, I thought it would be forever. I never envisioned myself as a single parent. I never saw myself divorced. After all, we were married 13 years.

It was January 21, 2013. I'll never forget it. I wanted to attend a book club event, and my husband was totally against it. We only had one car. I ended up in church at intercessory prayer. I remember getting over in a corner and crying out to God to take my life. I didn't want to live like this anymore. I felt like God had abandoned me. I remember thinking, *there has to be more to life than this*. I was praying to God, saying, "Lord, I'm your servant, your child. I'm an heir. If this is the best, it gets, just take my life now." I meant every word of it too. Then I heard God say, "That's enough! You are released from the marriage."

I know some would argue that God didn't say that, but I know what He said to me. The very next day, January 22, 2013, I walked away from the marriage. I didn't know how we would make it, but God saw fit to bring us through. My children and I were on our way to brighter days. I trust God. The journey continues.

Answered the Call

It is one thing to accept the Call, but when you answer the Call, everything changes. During my marriage, I had accepted my Call to preach the gospel. Yet, I spent a lot of time playing small in my Call because I had a husband who had to be seen as the head, so I spent a lot of time supporting him and making him look good.

After the divorce, I was devastated. I had to go on a real hunt to rediscover who Jamilla was and allow God to heal me, from the inside, of all the past hurt, pain, and shame of what I thought was another failed attempt in life. The devil threw all types of fiery darts at me to try to make me believe everything God had promised me was a lie. Looking back at that time, I almost believed him.

Despite my doubts, fears, disappointments, and mishaps, God kept proving himself over and over again. He continuously showed me that not only was He my God, He was also my Father. The one that would stick closer to me than any other. He reassured me that He had never left me or forsaken me.

I, finally, embraced the Call to preach and teach and walked in the gifting of the prophetic, fully and completely. It was then that life totally turned around for me. I surrendered all to God. I know it's hard for women in ministry, even more challenging for a divorced single mother. Yet, I stood on the promises of God for my life and that of my children.

Once I committed to the Call that was on my life, things turned around for me and my children. I took back my life. After losing three homes, having no money, being homeless, and leaving a dead-end marriage, there was nowhere to go but up from here.

Doors were opening, and I began to come alive again. I was preaching, teaching, and sharing what God had placed on the inside of me with others. Walking in my Call ignited something greater on the inside of me, my purpose. I started a women's group, ***"Sister's Let's Giv'em Something To Talk About."*** Connecting and sharing with women from all walks of life was reviving, refreshing, and rejuvenating.

We all have our own stories, our own journeys, but one common denominator is that we were all determined to become a better version of ourselves. As the organization continued to grow in number, so did the call, so did the assignment. Our women's group has grown over the years, and women are being blessed, empowered, transformed, and embracing their Call all because I said yes to mine and was positioned to incubate them to say yes to theirs.

I took back the control I once lost over my finances. I invested in the teachings of Dave Ramsey's "Financial Peace University" after mastering the teachings in my own life. I was then able to become an FPU coordinator, and I now teach others to do the same.

When you walk in your Call, not only do you change, but everything around you changes. Everything connected to you changes. It didn't just stop with my ministry and my money. Deciding to take my life back also enabled me to find love and embrace it. I am love, and I am loveable. That all came with much prayer and discovering who I was and who God was to me. I, now, wanted to share my love with a companion. I had to position myself to be "found" like the Bible says, "He who finds a wife, finds a good thing and obtains favor from the Lord (Proverbs 18:22).

God answered my prayers and sent me the man of my dreams, Darrell Johnson, the real love of my life! He became a great friend and is now my fiancé. Due to COVID-19 and all that took place in 2020, we pushed our wedding date back to 2022. We look forward to sharing our special day with our family and friends. Our love for each other has stood the test of time. He is my best friend, and I am his. Our ability to love despite our backgrounds, experiences, and differences makes it all worth the wait. I had experienced bad and had been down, so I immediately appreciated this good thing that came into my life and swept me off my feet. This love story is a whole book in itself. I surely hope to get to share it a much more detail one day. Saying yes to the

Call opened the door to it all. I'm living my best life, praise Jesus. The journey continues.

Pulse Check...

I know it's been a rollercoaster of a ride! Thanks for taking it with me thus far. It ain't over, but I promise you it gets better. As you reflect on what I've shared about me and my experiences, let's take a pause for the cause and take a pulse check. After having read about my journey so far, where are you right now in your thought process? I am sure reading about my journey has caused you to reflect on yours.

In what section of A.I.T. (Advanced Individual Training) did you really connect with? There is no right or wrong response here. This is a pulse check.

_____

_____

_____

_____

_____

_____

Relationships are complicated and uniquely different. No two are the same. Can you reflect back on a time in your relationship, whether present or past, that you have experienced life-altering events? What was it? What did you do? How did you handle it?

_____

_____

_____

_____

Knowing you have a Call/assignment on your life and answering it are two different scenarios. Have you identified with your Call/assignment? If so, how has answering it changed your life?

_____

_____

_____

_____

THE JOURNEY TO BECOMING THE

WELL-ARMED Woman

Duty Station

Understanding My Process

P rocess is defined as a series of actions or steps taken to achieve a particular end. When one understands their process, it makes the journey easier to navigate. My process began the day I was born. I just didn't know it then.

As my life unfolded and evolved, my process was defining itself. I can look back over my life and do one of two things: reminisce with regret or reminisce and reflect. You see, the Bible declares that "All things work together for good." It may not feel good, but it's working for my good. Some may ask, "How can a little girl growing up without her father being present in her life even though he lives in her neighborhood be good?" Others may ask, "How is a fifteen-year-old losing her mother and left to figure out this thing called life ultimately alone, good?" I could go on, but I think you get the point.

You see, while those events in my life didn't feel good, they ultimately worked for my good and shaped and molded the life of the well-armed woman you are reading about today. You will not catch me waddling in self-pity because I have come to understand that my journey was predestined, ordained. There is nothing that my mom or dad could have done differently because it was written. Not just my life, but your life as well.

When we understand that there is one greater who has chosen the path of life that we would ultimately travel and we embrace it, it makes transport less tiresome, less challenging. Once I embraced a heart check, I became totally surrendered to God's process for my life. This didn't happen until my forties, but it happened. Before that, I realized I had not come to the end of myself. I was still trying to navigate my own destiny. My inner me was the enemy.

Preparation in Basic Training, however, prepared me for the journey I would come to face in life. I learned tactics that prepared me, like hand-to-hand combat, how to fire a weapon, and how to defeat the enemy, even when the enemy was me. The discipline and focus on the target, my goal, provided me with strength, courage, and endurance build-up to overcome every obstacle. I can't give up, or I might die. My vision might die. My assignment might die. So even if I have to low-crawl, I must stay focused on my goals, my assignment, keep going, keep pressing.

I can recall going through an obstacle course in basic training. Before I even started, I knew two things: there was a beginning, and there was an end. Looking ahead at the course, I could sometimes see what was next and possibly strategize on overcoming it. Because this was such a lengthy obstacle course, I couldn't always see what was next. It was only until I approached the next obstacle that I could take a moment to strategize how to get over it. There were instances where I had to climb over something and instances where I had to crawl under something. There were times I ran and times I walked. Through all of this, each obstacle is required in action. I can remember the platoon going through it together. There were shouts of encouragement coming from others, but ultimately each individual had to cross the finish line for themselves.

Along with the encouragement were distractions. This event took place at night where bullets were flying over our heads. All of this was preparation for actual combat if we ever encountered it. So now survival mode kicks in! Complete the course without dying! Isn't it much like the process of life we endure? There's a beginning and an end. Along the way, obstacles are going to pop up that we must overcome. Some simple, and some more challenging. The only way to know what's next is to get through one obstacle at a time.

When we understand the process is necessary, we know that in order to get to our destination, we must go through the process. Don't fight the process, Sis. It's necessary. The journey continues.

Embracing My Assignment

Knowing you're called to do a thing and answering it is one thing. Embracing the assignment of the Call is another. I have come to a great place in my life. The love, peace, and joy I now have has allowed me to not only answer the Call but embrace the assignment of it. I live for it. I embody it, and it embodies me. I wake up for it. I show up for it. I seek out knowledge, education, and information to enhance it, understanding that my Call is my assignment. That my journey and everything I've endured had absolutely nothing to do with me and everything to do with God's will, plan, and purpose for my life.

I could have written, sung, and produced "Cry Me A River" after all I've been through. Instead, I chose to make the movie and sequel of the life I'm currently living out loud, evolving and advancing daily. I will not be defeated. I've come too far from where I started from.

When I started "Sisters, Let's Giv'em Something to Talk About," I had no idea the impact it would have, the lives it would touch. I didn't know that the women who connected to the vision would look forward to our monthly gatherings, and when COVID-19 hit, stay faithful to joining the Zooms. That wasn't because of me; it was in spite of me remaining faith and committed to the assignment on my life.

January 2021 was supposed to be the month we were going to hold our 2nd Women's Empowerment event, but due to COVID-19, we had to reschedule the event to August 2021. I could have gotten in my feelings and given in to defeat, but because I didn't, I wasn't defeated. The safety of everyone was at the forefront of my mind, and the smart thing to do was to reschedule, not cancel. There is a difference. The event will still take place. The women are even more excited.

So you see, sister, when your assignment has destiny attached to it, nothing can stop it! The embracement of my assignment has taken me out of my shell and exposed me to so many open doors and opportunities. I share "Motivational Mondays" and "Finance Fridays" on my Facebook page. Sharing inspiration, information, and nuggets that will transform the lives of those who will embrace the information.

Embracing your assignment is a choice; it requires sacrifice, sometimes sleepless nights, and a stick-to-it attitude! I believe in you, Sis! This is only the beginning! There's no stopping you now. You are on your own journey to becoming a well-armed woman! The journey continues.

Forward March

"Brethren, I count not myself to have apprehended: but this one thing I do, forgetting those things which are behind, and reaching forth unto those things which are before. I press toward the mark for the prize of the high calling of God in Christ Jesus." – Philippians 3:13-14.

Paul made it very clear here as he was talking to the church at Philippi that he was putting behind him the things of old. That he was pressing forward toward the mark, the prize, the destination, the purpose for which he was called in Christ Jesus.

We were all created for a purpose. There is a reason for each one of our lives—a problem we were created to solve. An invention we were created to invent. A life we were called to birth. A life we were called to impact. We will never do any of it looking back. We must use those experiences as fuel and stepping stools to attain the prize and reach the mark. They should never be the anchors that hold us back and keep us from moving forward.

In the military, there was a military command given of "Forward March." We were commanded to do just that, march forward. The loss of my mom, dad, half-brother, or my grandparents couldn't hold me back when I received the command. My first marriage couldn't hold me back when the orders were to march forward. Not even being a homeless single mom could hold me back when I received marching orders to move forward.

I may no longer be in the United States Army, but I am NOW a soldier in the Army of the Lord. God has commanded me to march forward. Leaving the past behind me, I press. I press through the struggles, challenges, and disappointments life bring. I press through the noise, the doubts, fears, and the uncertainties we face daily, trusting that the will and plan of God for my will prevail.

I, you, we, can never stop. Giving up is not an option. You may find that you have to mark-time march, which is another military command that means marching in place. WE NEVER STOPPED MOVING! You may have to slow down, go back to the drawing board, begin again, but you can never stop! Continue to mark-time march, if you must, but keep moving forward. Don't allow the opinions of others or your current or past situations keep you from advancing and going after your dreams or goals. You were created for this. Whatever your "this" is, Sis! Gird up your waist trainer, put on your Spanx, then put on the sharpest outfit in your closet and go get it!

Our journeys to becoming well-armed women will not look the same. Your coordinates will be different from mine, even if similar. Our processes won't look alike either. Yet, the one thing that we share, Sis, is the bounce-back spirit that won't allow us to stop, give up or give in.

We were created to win! We are more than conquerors. No matter what life throws at us, we will step up to the plate and swing that bat. We might not always hit a home run, but we must learn to celebrate the small victories. At least you got on first base.

Moving forward won't always come with a grand fan fair, parade, or a thousand post likes. What it will have is you, my sister, transitioning as you evolve into the well-armed woman you were, called, predestined, ordained, justified, and qualified to be. The whole armor of God is yours for the wearing. So, every morning before you get dressed in the natural, put on your war clothes in the spirit.

Ephesians 6:14-17 says, *"Stand therefore, having your loins gird about with truth, and having on the breastplate of righteousness; And your feet shod with the preparation of the gospel of peace; Above all, taking the shield of faith, wherewith ye shall be able to quench all the fiery darts of the wicked. And take the helmet of salvation, and the sword of the Spirit, which is the word of God."*

Sis, keep marching, keep moving forward. You are now armed and dangerous. A well-armed woman tried, trained, and ready for battle, but, STILL, the journey continues!

Journey Continues...

While it is true we have come this far by faith, there is still so much that lies ahead of us. So much more for us to do. Are you ready, Sis? The marathon continues, and so does our journey to becoming a well-armed woman. We are forever growing and evolving! There is still so much to be uncovered, discovered, and created by us.

Now that you understand your process and its purpose.
What will you do differently moving forward?

_____

_____

_____

You have been called to your assignment. There are so many others waiting for you to align with your purpose so they can walk in theirs. Write down three things that you will execute within the next 60-90 days that will advance your purpose as well as those that are depending on you.

_____

_____

_____

I would like to leave you with words of affirmation. No one else can do, be, have, or create what has been assigned to you to do. You, my sister, are wonderfully and beautifully made. You are the essence of creation. There is no creation without you, woman!

You are royalty. Nations and generations are your inheritance. If ever a mark was to be made in this world, no one can make it like you. You are strong. You are wise. You are brilliant. You are beautiful inside and out. When life throws you lemons, you create a lemonade franchise because you aren't selfish, so you provide an opportunity for others. Who is this Well-Armed Woman?

I AM _____

(Write Your Name)

AND The Journey Continues...

ABOUT THE *Author*

JAMILLA S. ROBERTSON

JAMILLA S. ROBERTSON

Jamilla is best known for being a minister of the gospel, a motivational powerhouse, a published author, an encouraging voice, a mom, a soon-to-be wife, and a great friend to many. She passionately believes that ministry starts at home. She also devotes a lot of time to her women's group, **Sisters, Let's Giv'em Something to Talk About**.

Her group meets on a monthly basis to encourage women to live a more fulfilled life, both spiritually and naturally. Jamilla is a faithful and devoted leader to the church she is currently affiliated with, Rise Church, Rocky Mount, NC. She is genuinely a humble servant of the Lord, and her story is proof that success is NOT about resources; it's about being resourceful and ambitious. It's about pressing forward despite life's challenges and nay-sayers.

Jamilla knows that her calling to serve as a motivational force will further push women to find out who they were created to be and for what reason they were put on this Earth in the first place. Earning the title "mid-wife" to many people, Jamilla continues to challenge women across the country to birth the visions that have been given to them. And she will NEVER stop!

Jamilla is a published author that teamed up with fellow author and powerhouse, Sharonette Smart, to bring you 31 days of intimate devotion with your Creator, **God's Concerned About What Concerns You**. The key ingredient to staying focused and remaining faithful through the process of life is staying connected to the Source. This 31-day devotion was specifically designed to help you overcome fear and trust God's process, knowing that GOD gave you the vision, and He also holds the Master Plan.

Her most recent accomplishment is that she has become a Financial Coordinator for Dave Ramsey's Financial Peace University. She has assisted many through financial freedom and becoming debt-free.

She currently resides in Rocky Mount, NC. She received her formal education from Edgecombe Community College and North Carolina Wesleyan College, where she has a bachelor's degree in Business Administration.

Connect with Jamilla:

@jamilla.s.robertson

@jamilla_givemsomethin2tlkabout

Email: jamillamotivatesu@gmail.com

Jamilla is available for:

- Guest Ministry
- Keynote Speaking
- Coaching
- Financial Workshop
- Self-Awareness Workshops
- Retreats
- Mistress of Ceremony

Connect/book today via her website:
www.jamillasrobertson.com

"You took my vision way farther than I ever expected! You have truly tapped into your gift & God is using it to bless many people."

Jamilla

getpublished@sheropublishing.com

SHEROPUBLISHING.COM

www.ingramcontent.com/pod-product-compliance
Lightning Source LLC
Chambersburg PA
CBHW061046110426
42740CB00049B/2469